NARRATIVES OF INDIAN CAPTIVITIES

The Dangers and Sufferings of Robert Eastburn and His Deliverance from Indian Captivity

Reprinted from the Original Edition of 1758 with Introduction and Notes by

John R. Spears

HERITAGE BOOKS
2016

HERITAGE BOOKS
AN IMPRINT OF HERITAGE BOOKS, INC.

Books, CDs, and more—Worldwide

For our listing of thousands of titles see our website
at
www.HeritageBooks.com

A Facsimile Reprint
Published 2016 by
HERITAGE BOOKS, INC.
Publishing Division
5810 Ruatan Street
Berwyn Heights, Md. 20740

Copyright © 1904 The Burrows Brothers Company

— Publisher's Notice —
In reprints such as this, it is often not possible to remove blemishes from the original. We feel the contents of this book warrant its reissue despite these blemishes and hope you will agree and read it with pleasure.

International Standard Book Numbers
Paperbound: 978-0-7884-4081-6
Clothbound: 978-0-7884-6430-0

CONTENTS

	PAGE
INTRODUCTION	7
EASTBURN NARRATIVE	21
Title-page (facsimile)	23
Preface	25
To the Reader	27
A Faithful Narrative, &c.	29
INDEX	73

INTRODUCTION

ROBERT EASTBURN, whose *Faithful Narrative* is one of the valuable, because one of the undoubted, original authorities relating to the war that destroyed the French power in North America, was captured by a force of French soldiers and Indians on a wagon road that crossed the divide between the Mohawk River and Wood Creek, just north of the modern city of Rome, New York. He was carried thence to Canada, where he was adopted into an Indian family, and where he remained, part of the time with the Indians, and a part with the French, for something less than two years.

It will add to the interest of the narration of his experiences to know that Eastburn was born in England in 1710 (see *Memoirs of the Rev. Joseph Eastburn*), but was brought to America by his parents when he was four years old. Thereafter his home was in Philadelphia. His parents were Quakers, but in 1739, Robert was won over to the Presbyterians by the preaching of George Whitefield,* and when Whitefield organized a congregation, Robert became one of its deacons. To those who are acquainted with the history of the American frontier during the eighteenth century, the fact that Eastburn was a Christian is of peculiar interest. For when captured by the French invaders he was one of a party of men who were on their way to the frontier post of Oswego to engage in the Indian trade; and no men, as a class, have been so utterly degraded and deeply cursed by their trade as those who have dealt with the aboriginal inhabitants of the earth. With them a thought of fair dealing

---

* Franklin, in his autobiography, says of Whitefield: " In 1739 arrived among us from Ireland the Reverend Mr. Whitefield, who had made himself remarkable there as an itinerant preacher. He was at first permitted to preach in some of our churches; but the clergy, taking a dislike to him, soon refused him their pulpits, and he was obliged to preach in the fields. The multitudes of all sects and denominations that attended his sermons were enormous, and it was matter of speculation to me, who was one of the number, to observe the extraordinary influence of his oratory on his hearers, . . notwithstanding his common abuse of them, by assuring them they were naturally *half beasts and half devils.* It was wonderful to see the change soon made in the manners of our inhabitants. From being thoughtless or indifferent about religion, it seemed as if all the world were growing religious." Under Whitefield's influence a church one hundred feet long by seventy feet broad was erected and paid for before dedication. It was " vested in trustees, expressly for the use of any preacher of any religious persuasion who might desire to say something to the people of Philadelphia."

was an evidence of weakness; the ability to overreach the savage was their constant boast. Nevertheless, because some were strictly honest, according to their light (Quakers and Moravians traded with the Indians), and because as a class the traders were most energetic, enterprising, and courageous, it seems likely that the story of their work and adventures should make the most interesting of the chapters of the American annals that have not yet been written.

Thus, it was the work of the Indian traders chiefly — their anxiety to preserve and extend the fur-trade — that caused all the long series of French and Indian raids on the British-American frontier during the period so graphically described by Parkman in his *Half Century of Conflict*. And the first stroke delivered on the American continent, in what is known as the "Seven Years' War" — the war during which Eastburn was captured — was struck by Charles Langlade, a French trader, with a party of Ottawas and Ojibways, who attacked the American traders and the Indians who were gathered at Pickawillany (near the modern Piqua, Ohio), June 21, 1752.

To show the courage and enterprise of Robert Eastburn as a trader, it is necessary to go over the events that, in America, preceded and led to the Seven Years' War.

Under the treaty of Utrecht (April 11, 1713), and that of Aix-la-Chapelle (October 7, 1748), the British had the right to trade with the Indians of the interior of North America, regardless of the claims of France to that territory. That every British trader would have made haste to exchange a pint of rum, or six cents' worth of red paint, for a beaver-skin at every opportunity, regardless of treaties, may be admitted; but the fact is they had the legal right to do it.

In pursuit of the profits thus to be obtained, the traders — particularly those of Philadelphia — thronged through the passes of the Alleghanies, after the treaty of Aix-la-Chapelle. In 1749, it is said (Parkman) that three hundred of them led their packhorses into the wilds of the Mississippi Valley. Governor Dinwiddie, of Virginia, said of them that "they appear to be in general a set of abandoned wretches," and Governor Hamilton, of Pennsylvania, concurred in that opinion. But whatever their morals they fearlessly threaded the forests of the region beyond the mountains, met and fought the rival traders of the north, went to the Indian villages wherever to be found, and in time established a station on Sandusky Bay, although the French had a station at Detroit and another on the Maumee River, in northern Ohio.

Commandant Raymond, in charge of the French post on the Maumee, wrote, at about this time:

"All the tribes who go to the English at Pickawillany come back loaded with gifts. . . If the English stay in this country we are lost. We must attack and drive them out."

The Indians that had settled around Detroit were invited to make the attack, but they were found to be "touched with disaffection;" and it was then that Charles Langlade came from the upper lakes and destroyed Pickawillany.

In the meantime the French had taken a formal "renewal of possession" of the Ohio country by sending Céloron de Bienville to bury certain lead plates in the Ohio watershed, and to nail tin plates, on which the French royal coat of arms had been painted, to a number of trees — all of which acts were duly attested by a notary public carried along for the purpose. The attack upon Pickawillany having proved as futile as the expedition of Céloron — though an Indian chief called "Old Britain" was boiled and eaten by Langlade's Indians — measures that were to prove strikingly effective for a time, were adopted by the French.

An expedition was sent by way of Erie, Pennsylvania, to the headwaters of the Alleghany River, where a post was established (1752), and named Le Bœuf. It stood where Waterford,

Pennsylvania, is now found. In the spring of 1753, they moved forward to the site of the modern Venango, and there prepared to descend to the junction of the Alleghany and Monongahela in the year after that.

It was now that Governor Dinwiddie, alarmed at what he deemed an invasion of Virginia, and at the prospect of a transfer of the horrors of the French and Indian border warfare from the frontier of New England to the borders of his own colony, sent the youthful George Washington to make a formal demand that the French leave. Legardeur de St. Pierre, commanding the French, replied, "I do not think myself obliged to obey."

Accordingly Dinwiddie raised three hundred "raw recruits," and sent them to occupy the favorable site for a fort that Washington had seen, meantime, at the forks of the Ohio. William Trent, a trader, and a gang of backwoodsmen went with them, and on an unnamed day in April, 1754, these backwoodsmen began building a fort where Pittsburg now stands.

Their work was apparently in vain. On April 17th, five hundred Frenchmen, with eighteen cannon, came down the Alleghany River, under Captain Claude Pecaudy de Contrecœur, and drove them away.

Washington's attack on the French force under Ensign Coulon de Jumonville (May 28,

1754) followed, and that is usually called the beginning, in America, of the Seven Years' War. Then by finesse, rather than by force of arms, the French, under Coulon de Villiers, drove Washington from Fort Necessity (July 4, 1755). Though as yet not formally declared, the great war was well on.

In the meantime (on February 20, of this year), the "trusty and well-beloved Edward Braddock," with two regiments of British soldiers, arrived at Hampton, Virginia. An intercolonial conference was held at Alexandria, beginning on April 14, to consider measures for the prosecution of the war, at which Governor William Shirley, whom Eastburn mentions, was present.

The plans made here included attacks on Acadia, Crown Point, Niagara, and Fort Duquesne, as the post at the forks of the Ohio was called. Shirley " and Dinwiddie stood in the front of the opposition to French designs;" to Shirley was assigned the work of capturing Niagara, and he was placed next in rank to Braddock, in the command of the British forces in America. Braddock himself undertook the task of marching through the wilderness to Fort Duquesne.

How Braddock, with 1,373 picked men, reached Turtle Creek, eight miles from Fort Duquesne, on July 7, crossed the Monongahela on the ninth, and was overwhelmed by an inferior force of

French and Indians on the site of the modern village of Braddock, Pennsylvania, a little later, need not be told here in detail. The important fact is that the French triumph was complete and seemingly decisive. They not only held control of the fort at the forks, but through the shameful retreat of the British to Philadelphia, the French were left in undisputed control of the passes of the Alleghanies. That the British confirmed their control of Acadia, in this season, by expelling certain French families from the territory; and that the forces under William Johnson checked the French under Baron Dieskau at Lake George, afforded the people of Pennsylvania and Virginia no consolation. For the evil that Governor Dinwiddie had foreseen was upon them. The horrors of the French and Indian wars that, for half a century, had desolated the frontiers of New England, now loomed over the Alleghanies.

"If you consider it necessary to make the Indians to act offensively against the English, his Majesty will approve of your using that expedient," said a letter dated September 6, 1754, from the French colonial minister to Governor Duquesne, of Canada. Duquesne thought that expedient necessary. Captain Dumas succeeded Contrecœur in the command of Fort Duquesne, and on July 24, 1756, wrote to the minister, saying:

"M. de Contrecœur had not been gone a week before I had six or seven different war parties in the field at once, always accompanied by Frenchmen. I have succeeded in ruining the three adjacent provinces, Pennsylvania, Maryland, and Virginia, driving off the inhabitants and totally destroying the settlements over a tract of country thirty leagues wide, reckoning from the line of Fort Cumberland."

And the Rev. Claude Godfroy Coquard, S.J., in a letter to his brother, said in reference to the work of these war parties (*N. Y. Col. MSS.*, vol. x., p. 528):

"The Indians do not make any prisoners; they kill all they meet, men, women, and children. Every day they have some in their kettle, and after having abused the women and maidens, they slaughter or burn them."

On one occasion a band of these Indians swooped down to within sixty miles of Philadelphia. A company of the harassed settlers, in their desperation, came in from the frontier, bringing with them the mutilated bodies of murdered friends and relatives, which they displayed at the doors of the Assembly chamber, while they bitterly cursed the opponents of an active war against the savage intruders.

It was in the midst of the red aggressions of the war parties sent out by Dumas that Robert Eastburn, a deacon in the First Presbyterian

Church of Philadelphia, left home with a party of traders (among them being his own son, a lad seventeen years old), and traveled away into the wilderness, bound to Oswego, the most advanced post of the American frontier — the one nearest to the triumphant French — to engage in the fur-trade with such Indians as he might find in that region. And he did that, too, when he knew that Oswego would be in imminent danger of attack while he was there, and that there was no small probability that his party would be intercepted while he was on the way, as, indeed, actually happened.

Robert Eastburn was, in fact, one of the many heroes of commerce, now well-nigh forgotten. It was characteristic of such a man to take his gun and join the soldiers, when a squad was sent out to hunt the enemy. And no one is surprised to learn that he was cool enough to bring down two at one shot, when the enemy were found.

The story of the fight in which Eastburn was captured is told, with some variations in the statements of facts, in volume x. of the *New York Colonial Manuscripts*. The account most nearly accurate is that in *Journal of Occurances in Canada from October, 1755, to June, 1756*. Parkman has the most interesting modern account in his *Montcalm and Wolfe*.

At the opening of the campaign of 1756, the

French held Ticonderoga, as well as Fort Duquesne, and all the borders of the Great Lakes, except the one post of Oswego. While yet the snow lay deep upon the ground in the northern part of New York, they learned from the Indians of the Iroquois tribes, who were more or less friendly to them, that the English contemplated sending an expedition, by way of Oswego and Lake Ontario, to attack Niagara, while another expedition would try to reduce Ticonderoga and Crown Point. The Indians also told the French that in pursuance of the English intention to attack Niagara, immense quantities of provisions had been sent forward toward Oswego, while the winter roads were good, and that many of these supplies were piled up in the storehouses at the carrying-place between the Mohawk and Wood Creek.

Accordingly Vaudreuil, who had meantime become governor of Canada, not only did what he could to strengthen Ticonderoga and Niagara, but he planned a counter-stroke for the destruction of the forts and stores at the Mohawk-Wood Creek carrying-place. He also planned an attack on Oswego, but that was to come later.

To raid the carrying-place, Vaudreuil sent Joseph Chaussegros de Léry, a distinguished Canadian officer (Vaudreuil was partial to the Canadian officers), with three hundred and sixty-two picked men — soldiers, rangers, and

Indians — from Montreal to the mission of Oswegatchie (now Ogdensburg), and thence by trails through the woods to the head of the Mohawk Valley. After great hardships, due to a lack of provisions and the rigor of the weather (March is a harsh month in the Adirondack region), this force arrived on the road leading from Fort William, at the head of navigation on the Mohawk, to Fort Bull, at the head of navigation on Wood Creek, at 5:30 o'clock on the morning of March 26, 1756. As it happened, they found there a party of twelve teamsters, including an unnamed negro, who were on their way with provisions and traders' goods to Fort Bull. These they attacked, and killed or captured all the party except the negro.

The negro escaped to Fort William and gave the alarm. The French, on questioning their prisoners, under threat of torture, learned that only a small garrison — thirty men — held Fort Bull, and De Léry determined to attack it. Nearly all the Indians in the party objected to this attack, being well satisfied with the plunder obtained from the teamsters, but De Léry, with a little brandy to rouse their courage, persuaded a dozen of them to go with him, and the rest of them to guard the road from Fort William, and then he marched to the attack.

As De Léry approached Fort Bull, some of the Indians whooped, and thus gave the alarm to the garrison, who closed their gate in time to shut out the French, but the French, by a dash forward, were able to secure positions at all the loopholes and prevent the garrison using them. De Léry then called on the garrison to surrender, but in spite of the advantages the French had secured, and in spite of inferior numbers, the heroic band replied with muskets and hand grenades.

The fight lasted for an hour. At the end of that time the French succeeded in chopping down the gate, and as it fell, they rushed in and massacred every person they could find. Two or three escaped death by hiding. The stores were destroyed and the fort was burned.

In the meantime Captain Williams, commanding at Fort William, had sent out a scouting party. Behind this party marched Deacon Eastburn, bearing a musket that had been carefully loaded and primed. And what the result of that movement was, Eastburn shall tell for himself.   JOHN R. SPEARS

EASTBURN NARRATIVE
PHILADELPHIA: WILLIAM DUNLAP, 1758

Title-page and text reprinted from a copy of the original edition in the Library of Congress, Washington, D. C.

A FAITHFUL NARRATIVE,

OF

The many *Dangers* and *Sufferings*, as well as wonderful *Deliverances* of ROBERT EASTBURN, during his late *Captivity* among the INDIANS: Together with some *Remarks* upon the *Country* of CANADA, and the *Religion*, and *Policy* of its *Inhabitants*; the whole intermixed with devout *Reflections*.

By *ROBERT EASTBURN*.

Published at the earnest REQUEST *of many* FRIENDS, *for the Benefit of the* AUTHOR.

With a recommendatory PREFACE, by the Rev. *GILBERT TENNENT*.

PSALM 124. 6, 7. *Blessed be the Lord, who hath not given us up as a Prey to their Teeth: our Soul is escaped, as a Bird out of the Snare of the Fowler: The Snare is broken, and we are escaped.*
PSALM 103. 2, 4. *Bless the Lord, O my Soul; and forget not all his Benefits: Who redeemeth thy Life from Destruction; who crowneth thee with loving Kindness, and tender Mercies.*

PHILADELPHIA:
Printed by WILLIAM DUNLAP, 1758.

Preface.

CANDID READER,
The Author (and Subject) of the enfuing Narrative (who is a Deacon of our Church, and has been fo for many Years) is of fuch an eftablifhed good Character, that he needs no Recommendation of others, where he is known: a Proof of which, was the general Joy of the Inhabitants of this City, occafioned by his Return from a miferable Captivity! Together with the Readinefs of divers Perfons, to contribute to the Relief of himfelf, and neceffitous Family, without any Requeft of his, or the leaft Motion of that Tendency!— But, feeing the following Sheets, are like to fpread into many Places, where he is not known, permit me to fay, That upon long Acquaintance, I have found him to be a Perfon of Candor, Integrity, and fincere Piety; whofe Teftimony, may with Safety, be depended upon; which give his Narrative the greater Weight, and may induce to read it with the greater Pleafure; The Defign of it is evidently Pious, the Matters contained in it, and Manner of handling them, will, I

hope, be efteemed by the Impartial, to be entertaining and improving: I heartily wifh it may, by the divine Benediction, be of great and durable Service. I am thy fincere Servant, in the Gofpel of Jefus Chrift.

GILBERT TENNENT.

PHILADELPHIA, *Jan* 19, 1758.

KIND READERS,
    On my Return from my Captivity, I had no Thoughts of publifhing any Obfervations of mine to the World, in this Manner; as I had no Opportunity to keep a Journal, and my Memory being broken, and Capacity fmall, I was difinclined to undertake it; but a Number of my Friends were preffing in their Perfwafions, that I fhould do it; with whofe Motion I complied, from a fincere Regard to God, my King, and Country, fo far as I know my own Heart: The following Pages contain, as far as I can remember, the moft material Paffages that happened within the Compafs of my Obfervation, while a Prifoner in Canada; the Facts therein related are certainly true, but the Way of reprefenting fome Things efpecially, is not fo regular, clear, and ftrong, as I could wifh; but I truft it will be fome Apology, that I am not fo much acquainted with Performances of this Kind, as many others; who may be hereby excited to give better Reprefentations of Things, far beyond my Knowledge.
    I remain Your unfeigned Well-Wifher,
                    and humble Servant,
                        ROBERT EASTBURN.

PHILADELPHIA, *Jan.* 19, 1758.

A Faithful Narrative, &c.

ABOUT Thirty Tradefmen, and myfelf, arrived at Captain Williams's Fort,* (at the Carrying Place) in our Way to Ofwego, the 26th of March, 1756; who informed me, that he was like to be cumbered in the Fort, and therefore advifed us to take the Indian-Houfe for our Lodging. About Ten o'Clock next Day, a Negro Man came running down the Road, and reported, That our Slaymen were all taken by the Enemy; Captain Williams, on hearing this, fent a Serjeant, and about 12 Men, to fee if it was true; I being at the Indian-Houfe, and not thinking myfelf fafe there, in Cafe of an

---

*This fort stood where Rome, New York, now stands. It was erected by Captain William Williams, of Sir William Pepperell's regiment, to guard the south, or Mohawk, end of the carrying-place between the Mohawk River and Wood Creek, in the route from Albany to Oswego. It was a palisaded enclosure with, presumably, a two-story, loopholed log-house at each of two corners, to give the garrison a commanding view of the enemy, in case of attack. The fort was destroyed by the English after the French captured Oswego, and a little later Fort Stanwix was built in its place, from plans drawn by James Montresor, director of engineers and lieutenant-colonel in the British army in 1758.

Attack, and being alſo ſincerely willing to ſerve my King and Country, in the beſt Manner I could in my preſent Circumſtances, aſked him if he would take Company? He replied, with all his Heart! Hereupon, I fell into the Rear, with my Arms, and marched after them; when we had advanced about a Quarter of a Mile, we heard a Shot, followed with doleful Cries of a dying Man, which excited me to advance, in order to diſcover the Enemy, who I ſoon perceived were prepared to receive us: In this difficult Situation, ſeeing a large Pine-Tree near, I repaired to it for Shelter; and while the Enemy were viewing our Party, I having a good Chance of killing two at a Shot, quickly diſcharged at them, but could not certainly know what Execution was done, till ſome Time after; our Company likewiſe diſcharged, and retreated: Seeing myſelf in Danger of being ſurrounded, I was obliged to Retreat a different Courſe, and to my great Surprize, fell into a deep Mire, which the Enemy, by following my Track in a light Snow, ſoon diſcovered, and obliged me to ſurrender, to prevent a cruel Death. (They ſtood ready to drive their Darts into my Body, in caſe I refuſed to deliver up my Arms.) Preſently after I was taken, I was ſurrounded by a great Number, who ſtripped me of my Cloathing, Hat, and Neckcloth (ſo that I had nothing left but a Flannel Veſt, without Sleeves) put a Rope on my Neck, bound my Arms faſt behind me, put a long Band round my Body, and a large Pack on my Back, ſtruck me on the Head (a ſevere Blow,) and drove me through the Woods before them: It is not eaſy to conceive, how diſtreſſing ſuch a Condition is! In the mean Time, I endeavoured with all my little remaining Strength, to lift up my Eyes to God, from whom alone I could with Reaſon expect Relief! Seventeen or Eighteen Priſoners, were ſoon added to our Number, one of which informed me, that the Indians were angry with me, and reported to ſome of their Chiefs, that I had fired on them, wounded one, and killed another; for which he doubted they would kill me. Hereupon I conſidered that the Hearts of all Men are in the Hand of God, and that one Hair of our Head cannot fall to the Ground without his Permiſſion: I had not as yet learned what Numbers the Enemy's Parties conſiſted of; there being only about 100 Indians who had lain in Ambuſh on the Road, to kill or take into Captivity all that paſſed between the two Forts. Here an Interpreter came to me, to enquire what Strength Capt. Williams had to defend his Fort? After a ſhort Pauſe, I gave ſuch a diſcouraging Anſwer (yet conſiſtent with Truth) as prevented their attacking it, and of Conſequence the Effuſion of much Blood; a gracious Providence, which I deſire ever to retain a grateful Senſe of; for hereby it evidently appeared, that

I was fuffered to fall into the Hands of the
Enemy, to promote the Good of my Countrymen,
to better Purpofe than I could, by continuing
with them; verily the Almighty is wife in
Council, and wonderful in Working.

In the mean Time, the Enemy determined to
deftroy Bull's Fort,* (at the Head of Wood-
Creek) which they foon effected, all being put to
the Sword, except five Perfons, the Fort burnt,
the Provifion and Powder deftroyed; (faving
only a little for their own Ufe) then they retired
to the Woods, and joined their main Body,
which inclufive, confifted of 400 French, and
300 Indians, commanded by one of the principal
Gentlemen † of Quebec; as foon as they got together (having a Prieft with them) they fell on
their Knees, and returned Thanks for their
Victory; an Example this, worthy of Imitation!
an Example which may make prophane pre-
tended Proteftants blufh, (if they are not loft to
all Senfe of Shame) who inftead of acknowl-
edging a God, or Providence, in their military
Undertakings, are continually reproaching him
with Oaths and Curfes; is it any Wonder, that

---

* Fort Bull was a mere palisade wall around store-houses.
It was garrisoned by thirty men from Shirley's regiment. De
Léry attacked it with two hundred and sixty-five men.

† The commander was Joseph Chaussegros de Léry, an
active Canadian officer, who saw service at Fort Duquesne and
Crown Point. He is not to be confounded with Gaspard
Chaussegros de Léry, chief engineer of Canada, who was
called " a great ignoramus."

the Attempts of fuch, are blafted with Difappointment and Difgrace!

The Enemy had feveral wounded Men, both French and Indians among them, which they carried on their Backs; befides which, about Fifteen of their Number were killed, and of us about Forty: it being by this Time near dark, and fome Indians drunk, they only marched about 4 Miles and encamped; the Indians untied my Arms, cut Hemlock Bowes, and ftrewed round the Fire, tied my Band to two Trees, with my Back on the green Bowes, (by the Fire) covered me with an old Blanket, and lay down acrofs my Band, on each Side, to prevent my Efcape, while they flept.

Sunday the 28th, rofe early, the Commander ordered a hafty Retreat towards Canada, for fear of General Johnfon;* in the mean Time, one of our Men faid, he underftood the French and Indians defigned to join a ftrong Party, and fall on Ofwego,† before our Forces there, could

---

* Sir William Johnson. On learning from the Indians that the enemy had come to the carrying-place, he hurried reinforcements up the Mohawk, but arrived too late to intercept them.

† Near the end of the seventeenth century Governor Bellomont, of New York, suggested that the French might be barred out of the Iroquois country by building a fort where Oswego, New York, now stands, but nothing was done in the matter until Governor Burnet built a " stone house of strength " there, with his private funds, in the spring of 1727. This house soon became a noted trading-station, for it proved a formid-

get any Proviſion or Succours; having, as they thought, put a Stop to our relieving them for a Time: When we encamped in the Evening, the Commanding-Officer ordered the Indians to bring me to his Tent, and aſked me, by an Interpreter, If I thought General Johnſon would follow them, I told him I judged not, but rather thought he would proceed to Oſwego (which was indeed my Sentiment, grounded upon prior Information, and then expreſſed to prevent the Execution of their Deſign.) He farther enquired, what was my Trade? I told him that of a Smith; he then perſwaded me, when I got to Canada, to ſend for my Wife, ' for ſaid he, you can, get a rich Living there;' but when he ſaw that he could not prevail, he aſked no more Queſtions, but commanded me to return to my Indian Maſter: Having this Opportunity of Converſation, I informed the General, that his Indian Warriors had ſtripped me of my Cloathing, and would be glad he would be good enough to order me ſome Relief; to which he replied, that I would get Cloaths when I came to Canada, which was cold Comfort to one almoſt frozen! On my Return, the Indians perceiving I was unwell, and could not eat their

---

able rival to the French stations intended to supply the wants of the Indians on the borders of the Great Lakes. When Montcalm captured the place (Saturday, August 14, 1756), one of the defending structures was known on the frontier as Fort Rascal, because of the character of the work done by its builders.

coarſe Food, ordered ſome Chocolate (which they had brought from the Carrying-Place) to be boiled for me, and ſeeing me eat that, appeared pleaſed. A ſtrong Guard was kept every Night; One of our Men being weakened by his Wounds, and rendered unable to keep Pace with them, was killed and ſcalped on the Road! — I was all this Time almoſt naked, traveling through deep Snow, and wading through Rivers cold as Ice!

After Seven Days March, we arrived at Lake Ontario, where I eat ſome Horſe-Fleſh, which taſted very agreeably, for to the hungry Man, as Solomon obſerves, every bitter Thing is ſweet (a). The French carried several of their wounded Men all the Way upon their Backs, and (many of them wore no Breeches in their Travels

---

ᵃ On the Friday before we arrived at the Lake, the Indians killed a Porcupine, which is in bigneſs equal to a large Racoon, with ſhort Legs, is covered with long Hair, intermixed with ſharp Quills, which are their Defence: It is indeed dangerous coming very near them, becauſe they caſt their Quills * (which are like barbed Irons or Darts) at any Thing that oppoſeth them, which when they peirce, are not eaſy to be drawn out; for, though their Points are ſharp and ſmooth, they have a kind of Beard, which makes them ſtick faſt: However, the Indians threw it on a large Fire, burnt off the Hair and Quills, roaſted and eat of it, with whom I had a Part.

---

* It is now known that porcupines do not cast or throw their quills, and are not able to do so, though commonly believed to do so, at Eastburn's time. Many a backwoodsman has eaten a porcupine. When young the flesh is as good as that of a 'possum, they say.

in this cold Seafon, they are ftrong, hardy Men.) The Indians had Three of their Party wounded, which they likewife carried on their Backs, I wifh there was more of this Hardnefs, fo neceffary for War, in our Nation, which would open a more encouraging Scene than appears at prefent! The Prifoners were fo divided, that but few could Converfe together on our March, and (which was ftill more difagreeable and diftreffing) an Indian, who had a large Bunch of green Scalps, taken off our Men's Heads, marched before me, and another with a fharp Spear behind, to drive me after him; by which Means, the Scalps were very often clofe to my Face, and as we marched, they frequently every Day gave the *Dead Shout*,* which was repeated as many Times, as there were Captives and Scalps taken! In the Midft of this gloomy Scene, when I confidered, how many poor Souls were hurried into a vaft Eternity, with Doubts of their Unfitnefs for fuch a Change, it made me lament and expoftulate in the Manner following; O Sin what haft thou done! what Defolation and Ruin haft thou brought into this miferable World? What am I, that I fhould be thus fpared! My Afflictions are certainly far

---

*Schoolcraft writes *Sa-sa-kuon* to give an idea of the dead shout. It was the whoop by which the Indians announced, when approaching a village, their victory, and the number of scalps and prisoners taken.

lefs than my Sins deferve! Through the exceeding Riches of divine Goodnefs and Grace, I was in this diftreffing Situation fupported and comforted, by thefe Paffages of facred Scripture, viz. That our light Afflictions, which laft but for a Moment, fhall work for us a far more exceeding and eternal Weight of Glory. And that, though no Afflictions are for the prefent joyous, but grievous; yet neverthelefs, they afterwards yield the peaceable Fruits of Righteoufnefs, to them who are exercifed thereby. And farther, that all Things fhall work together for Good, to them that love God; to them who are the Called, according to his Purpofe. But to return,

I May, with Juftice and Truth obferve, That our Enemies leave no Stone unturned to compafs our ruin; they pray, work, and travel to bring it about, and are unwearied in the Purfuit; while many among us fleep in a Storm, that has laid a good Part of our Country defolate, and threatens the Whole with Deftruction: O may the Almighty awake us, caufe us to fee our Danger, before it be too late, and grant us Salvation! O that we may be of good Courage, and play the Man, for our People, and the Cities of our God! But alas, I am obliged to turn my Face towards cold Canada, among inveterate Enemies, and innumerable Dangers! O Lord, I pray thee, be my fafe Guard; thou haft already covered me in the Hollow of thy Hand; when Death caft Darts all around me, and many fell on every Side, I beheld thy Salvation! April 4th, Several French Battoes met us, and brought a large Supply of Provifion; the Sight of which caufed great Joy, for we were in great Want; then a Place was foon erected to celebrate Mafs in, which being ended, we all went over the Mouth of a River, where it empties itfelf into the Eaft-End of Lake Ontario, a great Part of our Company fet off on Foot towards Ofwegotchy;* while the reft were ordered into Battoes, and carried towards the Entrance of St Lawrence (where that River takes its Beginning) but by reafon of bad Weather, Wind, Rain, and Snow, whereby the Waters of the Lake were troubled, we were obliged to lie-by, and hall our Battoes on Shore; here I lay on the cold Shore two Days. Tuefday fet off, and entered the Head of St. Law-

---

Oswegotchie. It was a settlement of Iroquois Indians who had been converted by Abbé Piquet, a French missionary. It was established in 1749 where Ogdensburg, New York, now stands, and it was intended for the promotion of French political and trade interests, as well as the propagation of religion. Piquet called it "La Présentation." In 1753 it contained a palisaded fort, "flanked with block houses; a chapel, a storehouse, a barn, a stable, ovens, a sawmill, broad fields of corn and beans, and three villages of Iroquois, containing in all 49 bark lodges each holding three or four families, . . and as time went on this number was increased." —*Parkman.* The fort was armed with five two-pounder cannon and garrisoned with a squad of French soldiers.

rence, in the Afternoon; came too late at Night, made Fires, but did not lie down to sleep; embarked long before Day, and after some Miles Progress down the River, we saw many Fires on our Right-Hand, which were made by the Men who left us, and went by Land; with them we staid till Day, and then again embarked in our Battoes; the Weather was very bad (it snowed fast all Day) near Night arrived at Oswegotchy; I was almost starved to Death, but hoped to stay in this Indian Town till warm Weather; slept in an Indian Wigwam, rose early in the Morning (being Thursday) and soon to my Grief discovered my Disappointment! Several of the Prisoners had Leave to tarry here, but I must go 200 Miles farther down Stream, to another Indian Town; the Morning being extreamly cold, I applied to a French Merchant (or Trader) for some old Rags of Cloathing, for I was almost naked, but to no Purpose!

About Ten o'Clock, was ordered into a Battoe, on our Way down the River, with 8 or 9 Indians, one of which was the Man wounded in the Skirmish before mentioned; at Night we went on Shore, the Snow being much deeper than before, we cleared it away, and made a large Fire; here, when the wounded Indian cast his Eyes upon me, his old Grudge revived, he took my Blanket from me, and commanded me to dance round the Fire Bare-foot, and sing the

Prifoners Song, which I utterly refufed; this furprized one of my fellow Prifoners, who told me they would put me to Death (for he underftood what they faid) he therefore tried to perfuade me to comply, but I defired him to let me alone, and was through great Mercy, enabled to reject his Importunity with Abhorrence! The Indian alfo continued urging, faying, you fhall dance and fing; but apprehending my Compliance finful, I determined to perfift in declining it at all Adventures, and to leave the Iffue to the divine Difpofal! The Indian perceiving his Orders difobeyed, was fired with Indignation, and endeavoured to pufh me into the Fire, which I leapt over, and he being weak with his Wounds, and not being affifted by any of his Brethren, was obliged to defift: For this gracious Interpofure of Providence, in preferving me both from Sin and Danger, I defire to blefs God while I live!

Friday Morning, was almoft perifhed with Cold. Saturday, proceeded on our Way, and foon came in Sight of the upper Part of the Inhabitants of Canada; here I was in great Hopes of fome Relief, not knowing the Manner of the Indians, who do not make many Stops among the French, in their return from War, till they get Home: However when they came near fome rapid Falls of Water, one of my fellow Prifoners, and feveral Indians, together with myfelf, were put on Shore, to travel by Land, which pleafed me well, it being much warmer running on the Snow, than lying ftill in the Battoe; we paft by feveral French Houfes, but ftopt at none; the Veffel going down a rapid Stream, it required hafte to keep Pace with her, we croffed over a Point of Land, and found the Battoe waiting for us, as near the Shore as the Ice would permit: Here we left St. Lawrence and turned up Conafadauga River (b) but it being frozen up, we hauled our Battoe on Shore, and each of us took our Share of her Loading on our Backs, and marched

---

b The River St. Lawrence, at Lake Ontario, takes its Beginning through feveral Iflands, by which we are in no neceffity of coming within Sight of Frontenac, when we go down the River; it is fmooth Water from thence to Ofwegotche (or as it is called by the French *Legalet*) but from hence to Montreal, the Water is more fwift, with a Number of rapid Streams, though not dangerous to pafs through with fmall Boats and Bark Canoes, provided the Stearfmen are careful, and acquainted with the Places. In tranfporting Provifion and warlike Stores up Stream from Canada to Lake Ontario, there is a neceffity of unloading Battoes at feveral of the rapid Streams, and hauling them empty through fhoal Water near the Shore; and carrying the Loading by Land to where the Water is more Slack; though there be feveral of thefe Places, yet the Land Carriage is not very far: The Land on both Sides the River, appears fertile a great Part of the Way from the Lake to Montreal; but the nearer the Latter the worfe, more mirey and ftony: The Timber is White Pine, Afh, Maple, Beach, Hickory, Hemlock, Spruce; and from the Lake about 150 Miles down, plenty of White Oak, but none about Montreal of that Kind.

towards Conaſadauga.* an Indian Town, which was our deſigned Port, but could not reach it that Night; Came to a French Houſe, cold, weary, and hungry; here my old Friend, the wounded Indian, again appeared, and related to the Frenchman, the Affair of my refuſing to dance, who immediately affiſted the Indian to ſtrip me of my Flannel Veſt, before mentioned, which was my All: Now they were reſolved to compel me to dance and ſing! The Frenchman was as violent as the Indian, in promoting this Impoſition; but the Women belonging to the Houſe, ſeeing the rough Uſage I had, took pity on me, and reſcued me out of their Hands, till their Heat was over, and prevailed with the Indian to excuſe me from dancing; but he inſiſted that I muſt be ſhaved, and then he would let me alone (I had at that Time a long Beard, which the Indians hate) with this Motion I readily complied, and then the Indian ſeemed content.

Sunday, April 11th, Set off towards Conaſadauga, traveled about two Hours, and then ſaw

---

*A mission settlement of Indians containing a village of Iroquois and another of Algonquins. It was called also the Lake of the Two Mountains mission. The site is " a point on the St. Lawrence, just at the [west] extremity of the island of Montreal, where the river widens into a kind of lake. Two slight eminences, which soon obtained the name of mountains, gave it its name. Near these the mission was begun in 1720."— Shea's *American Catholic Missions.*

the Town, over a great River, which was ftill frozen; the Indians ftoped, and we were foon joined with a Number of our own Company, which we had not feen for feveral Days: The Prifoners, in Number Eight, were ordered to lay down our Packs, and be painted; the wounded Indian painted me, and put a Belt of Wampum round my Neck, inftead of the Rope which I had worn 400 Miles. Then fet off towards the Town on the Ice, which was four Miles over; our Heads were not allowed to be covered, left our fine Paint fhould be hid, the Weather in the mean Time very cold, like to Freeze our Ears; after we had advanced nearer to the Town, the Indian Women came out to meet us, and relieved their Hufbands of their Packs.

As foon as we landed at Conafadauga, a large Body of Indians came and incompaffed us round, and ordered the Prifoners to dance and fing the Prifoners Song, (which I was ftill enabled to decline) at the conclufion of which, the Indians gave a Shout, and opened the Ring to let us run, and then fell on us with their Fifts, and knocked feveral down; in the mean Time, one ran before to direct us to an Indian Houfe, which was open, and as foon as we got in, we were beat no more; my Head was fore with beating, and pained me feveral Days. The Squaws were kind to us, gave us boiled Corn and Beans to eat, and Fire to warm us, which was a great Mercy, for I was both cold and hungry: This Town lies about 30 Miles North-Weft from Montreal, I ftaid here till the Ice was gone, which was about Ten Days, and then was fent to Cohnewago, in Company with fome Indians, who when they came within Hearing, gave Notice by their Way of fhouting, that they had a Prifoner, on which the whole Town rofe to welcome me, which was the more diftreffing, as there was no other Prifoner in their Hands; when we came near Shore, a ftout Indian took hold of me, and hauled me into the Water, which was Knee-deep, and very cold: As foon as I got a-fhore, the Indians gathered round me, and ordered me to dance and fing, now when I was ftiff with Cold and Wet, and lying long in the Cannoe; here I only ftamped to prepare for my Race, and was incompaffed with about 500 Indians, who danced and fung, and at laft gave a Shout, and opened the Circle; about 150 young Lads made ready to Pelt me with Dirt and gravel Stones, and on my fetting off gave me a ftout Volley, without my fuffering great Hurt; but an Indian feeing me run, met me, and held me faft, till the Boys had ftored themfelves again with Dirt and fmall Stones, and let me run; but then I fared much worfe than before, for a fmall Stone among the Mud hit my Right-Eye, and my Head and Face were fo covered with Dirt, that I could fcarce fee my Way; but difcovering a Door of an Indian Houfe ftanding open, I run in: From this Retreat I was foon hauled, in order to be pelted more; but the Indian Women being more merciful interpofed, took me into a Houfe, brought me Water to wafh, and gave me boiled Corn and Beans to eat. The next Day, I was brought to the Center of the Town, and cried according to the Indian Cuftom, in order to be fent to a Family of Indians, 200 Miles up Stream, at Ofwegotchy, and there to be adopted, and abufed no more: To this End, I was delivered to three young Men, who faid I was their Brother, and fet forward on our Way to the aforefaid Town, with about 20 more Indians, but by reafon of bad Weather, we were obliged to encamp on a cold, ftony Shore, three Days, and then proceeded on; called at Conafadauga, ftaid there about a Week, in which Time, I went and viewed four Houfes at a Diftance from the Town, about a Quarter of a Mile from each other; in which, are reprefented in large Paint Work, the Sufferings of our Saviour, with Defign to draw the Indians to the Papift's Religion; the Work is curioufly done: A little farther ftand three Houfes near together, on the Top of a high Hill, which they call *Mount Calvary*,* with three large Croffes before them,

---

* Abbé Piquet, who established the mission at Oswegatchie, erected this Calvary and Way of the Cross. It " is even now a pilgrimage worthy of attention."—*Shea.*

which compleat the whole Reprefentation: To all thefe Houfes, the Priefts and Indians repair, in performing their grand Proceffions, which takes up much Time (c).

Set off on our Journey for Ofwegotchy, againft a rapid Stream, and being long in it, and our Provifion growing fhort, the Indians put to Shore a little before Night; my Lot was to get Wood, others were ordered to get Fires, and fome to Hunt; our Kettle was put over the Fire with fome pounded Indian Corn, and after it had boiled about two Hours, my oldeft Indian Brother, returned with a She Beaver, big with Young, which he foon cut to Pieces, and threw into the Kettle, together with the Guts, and took the four young Beavers, whole as they came out from the Dam, and put them likewife into

---

^c The pains the Papifts take to propagate such a bloody and abfurd Religion as theirs, is truly amazing! This brings to my Remembrance, the following Difcourfe, I had with two French Priefts in my Captivity; one of them asked me, if I was a Catholic; apprehending he meant the Romifh Religion, I anfwered no; he replied, *no Bon.* On my relating the above to a fellow Prifoner, he faid, I had anfwered wrong, becaufe by the Word *Catholic* he meant a Chriftian: Some Time after, I was again asked by the other Prieft, if I was a Catholic, I anfwered yes, but not a Roman Catholic; at which he fmiled, and asked, if I was a Lutheran. I replied, no; he again inquired whether I was a Calvanift, I told him I was; to which he faid, with warmth, *no Bon! no Bon!* which fignifieth, it is not good, it is not good. O! may not the Zeal of Papifts, in propagating Superftition and Idolatry, make Proteftants afhamed of their Lukewarmnefs, in promoting the Religion of the Bible!

the Kettle, and when all was well boiled, gave each one of us a large Difhfull of the Broth, of which we eat freely, and then Part of the old Beaver, the Tail of which was divided equally among us, there being Eight at our Fire; the four young Beavers were cut in the Middle, and each of us got half of a Beaver; I watched an Opportunity to hide my Share (having fatisfied myfelf before that tender Difh came to Hand) which if they had feen, would have much difpleafed them. The other Indians catched young Mufk-Rats, run a Stick through their Bodies, and roafted, without being fkinned or gutted, and fo eat them. Next Morning haftened on our Journey, which continued feveral Days, till we came near Ofwegotchy, where we landed about three Miles from the Town, on the contrary Side of the River; here I was to be adopted, my *Father* and *Mother* that I had never feen before were waiting, and ordered me into an Indian Houfe, where we were directed to fit down filent for a confiderable Time, the Indians appeared very fad, and my Mother began to cry, and continued crying aloud for fome Time, and then dried up her Tears, and received me for her Son, and took me over the River to the Indian Town; the next Day I was ordered to go to Mafs with them, but I refufed once and again, yet they continued their Importunity feveral Days, faying it was good to go to Mafs, but I ftill refufed;

and seeing they could not prevail with me, they seemed much displeased with their new Son (d). I was then sent over the River, to be employed in hard Labour, as a Punishment for not going to Mass, and not allowed a Sight of, or any Conversation with my fellow Prisoners; the old Indian Man that I was ordered to work with, had a Wife, and some Children, he took me into the Woods with him, and made Signs that I must chop, giving me an Ax, the Indian soon saw that I could handle the Ax: Here I tried to reconcile myself to this Employ, that they might have no Occasion against me, except concerning the Law of my God; the old Man began to appear kind, and his Wife gave me Milk and Bread when we came Home, and when she got Fish, gave me the Gills to eat, out of real Kindness; but perceiving I did not like them, gave me my own choice, and behaved lovingly! Here I saw that God could make Friends of

---

d When I was at Oswegotchy, the Indians took Notice, that I frequently retired alone, and supposing I had some bad Design, threatened if I did not desist, they would Tomahawk me; but my fellow Prisoner, who understood their Language, told them it would be a pity to hurt me on that Account, for I only went into a private Place to pray, which was true; the Indians replied, if so, it was good; but being yet suspicious, took Pains, by watching to find out how the Case was, and when they satisfied themselves, seemed pleased! and did not offer to interrupt me any more, which was a great Mercy; as the Contrary would have in some Degree, marred my Converse with God.

cruel Enemies, as he once turned the Heart of angry Eſau into Love and Tenderneſs; when we had finiſhed our Fence, which had employed us about a Week, I ſhewed the old Squaw my Shirt (having worn it from the Time I was firſt taken Priſoner, which was about ſeven Weeks) all in Rags, Dirt, and Lice; ſhe ſaid it was not good, and brought me a new One, with ruffled Sleeves (ſaying that is good) which I thankfully accepted. The next Day they carried me back to the Indian Town, and admitted me to converſe with my fellow Priſoners, who told me we were all to be ſent to Montreal, which accordingly came to paſs.

Montreal, at our Arrival here, we had our Lodging firſt in the Jeſuit's Convent, where I ſaw a great Number of Prieſts, and People that came to Confeſſion; after ſome ſtay, we were ordered to attend, with the Indians, at a Grand Council, held before the head General Vaudriel;* we Priſoners ſat in our Rank (ſurrounded with our Fathers and Brethren) but were aſked no Queſtions: the General had a Number of Officers to attend him in Council, where a noted Prieſt, called Picket,† ſat at his Right-Hand,

---

*Pierre François de Rigaud, Marquis de Vaudreuil-Cavagnal. He was governor of Canada from the summer of 1755 till the French lost the country, 1759.

† Abbé François Piquet. He was one of the most patriotic and zealous priests in French America. Though best known as the founder of Oswegatchie, his work at the Lake of the

who underſtands the Indian Tongue well, and does more Hurt to the Engliſh, than any other of his Order in Canada (his Dwelling is at Oſwegotchy). Here I was informed that ſome Meaſures were concerted to deſtroy Oſwego, which they had been long preparing to execute; we in our Journey met many Battoes going up Stream, with Proviſion and Men for an Attack on our Frontiers, which confirmed the Report: The Council adjourned to another Day, and then broke up. My Indian Father and Mother took me with them to ſeveral of their old Acquaintance, who were French, to ſhew them their lately adopted Son; theſe Perſons had been concerned with my Father and other Indians, in deſtroying many Engliſh Families in their younger Days; and (as one ſtanding by who underſtood their Language, ſaid,) were boaſting of their former Murders! After ſome Days the Council was again called, before which, ſeveral of the Oneida Chiefs appeared, and offered ſome Complaint againſt the French's attacking our Carrying-Place, it being their Land; but the

---

Two Mountains was notable in the annals of the Church. He was stationed at Fort Frontenac, at one time. When Montcalm captured Oswego, Piquet was present, and erected a huge cross to commemorate the French victory. He accompanied a number of raiding parties that invaded the British settlements. His energy was untiring. Though called vain and boastful, it is certain that he was ever ready to back his words with deeds.

General laboured to make them eafy, and gave them fundry Prefents of Value, which they accepted (e): After which, I knowing thefe Indians were acquainted with Captain Williams, at the Carrying-Place, fent a Letter by them, to let my Family and Friends know I was yet alive, and longed for Redemption; but it never came to Hand. The Treaty being ended, the General fent about ten Gallons of red Wine to the Indians, which they divided among us; after

---

^e The French in Canada, well knowing the great Importance of having the Indians in their Intereft, to promote their ambitious and unjuft Defigns, ufe a variety of Methods with them, among which, the following one is excellent in itfelf, and well worthy of Imitation, viz. They are exceeding careful to prevent fpirituous Liquors being fold to the Indians, and if any of the Inhabitants are proved guilty of it, their temporal Intereft is quite broke, and corporal Punifhment inflicted on them; unlefs the General, on fome particular Occafion, orders his Commiffioners to deliver fome to them. I may add, that knowing their Number is fmall, compared with the Britifh Inhabitants on this Continent, and muft quickly fall into their Hands, in cafe we united, and entered boldly into the Heart of their Country with a fufficient Force; for that very Reafon, they choofe to keep us continually on the Defencive, by fending when Occafion requires, large Bodies of Regulars, together with great Numbers of Indians, upon long and tedious Marches, that we may not come near their Borders; and efpecially by employing the Latter, conftantly to wafte and ravage our Frontiers, by which we are murdered by Inches, and beat without a Battle! By what I could learn when I was among them, they do not fear our Numbers, becaufe of our unhappy Divifions, which they deride, and from them, ftrongly expect to conquer us entirely! which may a gracious God, in Mercy, prevent!

came the Prefents, confifting of Coats, Blankets, Shirts, Skins (to make Indian Shoes) Cloth (to make Stockings) Powder, Lead, Shot, and to each a Bag of Paint, for their own Ufe, &c. After we Prifoners had our Share, my Mother came to me with an Interpreter, and told me I might ftay in the Town, at a Place fhe had found for me, if I pleafed (this was doubtlefs the Confequence of my declining to obey her Orders, in fome Inftances that affected my Confcience) this Propofal I almoft agreed to; but one of my fellow Prifoners, with whom I had before fome Difcourfe, about making our Efcape from the Indian Town, oppofed the Motion, and faid, "pray do not ftay, for if you do, we fhall not be able to form a Plan for our Deliverance;" on which I told her I chofe to go Home with her, and foon fet off by Land in our Way thither, to Lafcheen,* diftant from

---

* La Chine was the name given by envious competitors to the frontier trading-post, established by La Salle, soon after his arrival (1666) in New France. It stood at the head of the rapids above and nine miles from Montreal. It was the most dangerous, and probably it was then the most profitable post in America. Having learned from Seneca Indians that a river heading in their country flowed to a great salt sea, far away to the south, La Salle supposed it emptied into the South Sea, and that he might, by following that route, reach China. With unsurpassed courage and enterprise he mortgaged his trading-post, though it was yielding him large profits, to raise funds for the exploration of this river. He succeeded in following it as far as the falls of the Ohio (Louisville, Kentucky), and then, because his men deserted him, he was obliged to

Montreal about 9 Miles, where we left our Cannoes, and then proceeded, without Delay, on our Journey; in which I faw, to my Sorrow, great Numbers of Soldiers, and much Provifions, in Motion towards Lake Ontario.

After a painful and diftreffing Journey, we arrived at Ofwegotchy, where we likewife faw many Battoes, with Provifion and Soldiers, daily paffing by in their Way to Frontenac,* which greatly diftreffed me for Ofwego! Hence I refolved, if poffible, to give our People Notice of their Danger: To this End, I told two of my fellow Prifoners, that it was not a Time to fleep, and afked if they would go with me, to this they heartily agreed; but we had no Provifion, were clofely eyed by the Enemy, and could not lay up a Stock out of our Allowance: However, at this Time, Mr. Picket (before mentioned) had concluded to dig a large Trench round the Town; I therefore went to a Negro,

---

return, ruined, to Montreal. He had gone to find China; he returned to find the mortgage on his post at the rapids foreclosed. His old rivals, to deride him, began to call his lost post China — *La Chine* — and the name remains to this day, perpetuating the story of La Salle's first expedition into the wilds of America, and the ill nature of his competitors.

* Frontenac was the name (called also Cataraqui) of the fort, trading-post, and settlement established (1673) by La Salle and Count de Frontenac, where Kingston, Ontario, now stands. It was the first of the chain of forts intended to extend from Montreal to New Orleans that La Salle planned to secure the interior of the continent to the French crown.

the principal Manager of this Work (who could fpeak Englifh, French, and Indian, well) and afked him, if he could get Employ for two others, and myfelf, which he foon did; for which we were to have Meat and Wages. Here we had a Profpect of procuring Provifion for our Flight; this, I in fome Time effected for myfelf, and then afked my Brethren if they were ready, who replied they were not yet, but faid, Ann Bowman, our fellow Prifoner, had brought 130 Dollars from Bull's Fort, and would give them all they had Need of; I told them it was not fafe to difclofe fuch a Secret to her, but they blamed me for my Fears, and applied to her for Provifion, letting her know our Intention, who immediately informed the Prieft of it; on which we were apprehended, the Indians apprifed of our Defign, and a Court called; by Order of which, four of us were confined under a ftrong Guard, in a Room within the Fort, for feveral Days.

From hence, another and myfelf were fent to Cohnewago, under a ftrong Guard of 60 Indians, to prevent my ploting any more againft the French, and banifh all Hope of my Efcape! However, when we arrived at this Place, it pleafed that gracious God, who has the Hearts of all Creatures in his Hand, to incline the Captain of the Guard, to fhew me great Kindnefs, in giving me Liberty to walk or work where I pleafed, within any fmall Diftance; on which

I went to work with a French Smith, for fix Livers and five Soufe per Week; which the Captain let me have to myfelf, and farther favoured me with the Priviledge of Lodging at his Mother's Houfe, an Englifh Woman (named Mary Harris,* taken Captive when a Child, from Dearfield, in New-England) who told me fhe was my Grand-mother, and was kind; but the Wages being fmall, and not fufficient to procure fuch Cloathing as I was in Want of, I proceeded no farther with the French Smith, but went to my Uncle Peter, and told him I wanted Cloaths, and that it would be better to let me go to Montreal, and work there, where I could Cloath myfelf better, than by ftaying with him, and that without any Charge to him, who after fome Reafoning confented.

Set off on my Journey to Montreal, and on my entring the City met an Englifh Smith, who took me to work with him; after fome Time, we fettled to work in a Shop, oppofite to the General's Door, where we had the Opportunity of feeing a great Part of the Forces of Canada (both Soldiers and Indians) who were commonly brought there, before their going out to War; and likewife all Prifoners, by which

* Mary Harris was one of a considerable number of captured New England children who learned to prefer the Indian way of living to that of civilized people. According to Parkman, a tributary of the Muskingum River, in Ohio, was named White Woman's Creek, in her honor.

Means we got Intelligence how our People were preparing for Defence; but no good News from Oſwego, which made me fear, knowing that great Numbers of French were gone againſt it, and hearing of but few to defend it. Prayers were put up in all the Churches of Canada, and great Proceſſions made, in order to procure Succeſs to their Arms, againſt poor Oſwego; but our People knew little of their Danger, till it was too late: Certainly if more frequent and earneſt Application (both in private and public) was made to the God of Battle, we might with greater Probability, expect Succeſs would crown our military Attempts! To my Surprize, the diſmal News came, that the French had taken one of the Oſwego Forts; in a few Hours, in Confirmation of this, I ſaw the Engliſh Standards (the melancholly Trophy of Victory) and the French rejoicing at our downfal, and mocking us poor Priſoners, in our Exile and Extremity, which was no great Argument either of Humanity, or true Greatneſs of Mind; great Joy appeared in all their Faces, which they expreſſed by loud Shouts, firing of Cannon, and returning Thanks in their Churches; but our Faces were covered with Shame, and our Hearts filled with Grief! - - Soon after, I ſaw ſeveral of the Officers brought in Priſoners, in ſmall Parties, and the Soldiers in the ſame Manner, and confined within the Walls, in a ſtarving Condition, in order to make them Work, which fome complied with, but others bravely refufed; and laſt of all came the Tradefmen, among whom was my Son, who looking round faw his Father, who he thought had long been dead; this joyful Sight fo affected him, that he wept!—nor could I, in feeing my Son, remain unconcerned!— no; the Tendernefs of a Father's Bowels, upon fo extraordinary an Occafion, I am not able to exprefs, and therefore muſt cover it with a Vail of Silence!—But he, with all my Philadelphia Friends, being guarded by Soldiers, with fixed Bayonets, we could not come near each other, they were fent to the common Pound; but I haſtened to the Interpreter, to try if I could get my Child at Liberty, which was foon effected! When we had the Happinefs of an Interview, he gave me fome Information of the State of our Family, and told me, as foon as the News were fent Home, that I was killed, or taken, his Mother was not allowed any more Support from my Wages, which grieved me much, and added to my other Afflictions (f)!

ᶠ In the mean Time, it gave me fome Pleafure, in this Situation, to fee an Expreffion of equal Duty and Prudence in my Sons Conduct, who, though young in Years (about 17) and in fuch a confufed State of Things, had taken care to bring, with much Labour and Fatigue, a large Bundle of confiderable Value to me, it being Cloathing, &c. which I was in great Need of; he likewife faved a Quantity of Wampum, which we brought from New-York, and afterwards fold here, for 150 Livers. He traveled with me Part of the Journey towards

When the People taken at Ofwego, were fetting out on their Way to Quebec, I made Application for Liberty to go with them; but the Interpreter replied, that I was an Indian Prifoner, and the General would not fuffer it, till the Indians were fatisfied; and as they lived Two Hundred Miles from Montreal, it could not be done at that Time: Finding that all Arguments, farther on that Head, would not avail, becaufe I was not included in the Capitulation; I told the Interpreter, my Son muft go and leave me! in order to be ready at Quebec to go Home, when the Ofwego People went, which probably would be foon; he replied, "It would

Ofwego, but not being fo far on his Way, as I was when taken, he did not then fall into the Enemy's Hands, but continued free till Ofwego was taken, and was then remarkably delivered from the Hands of the Indians, in the following Manner, 15 young Lads were drafted out to be delivered to them (which from their known Cuftom, it is reafonable to conclude, was to fill up the Number they had loft in the Battle*) among which he was one: This barbarous Defign, which is contrary to the Laws of War, among all civilized Nations, the French artfully concealed, under the Pretext of fending them to work in the Battoes; but my Child taking Notice, that all that were chofen were fmall Lads, doubted their real Intention was bad,

*In Delafield's biography of Francis Lewis (one of the prisoners captured at Oswego) is this paragraph (p. 20): "Montcalm allowed his Indian allies to select thirty prisoners as their share of the booty, and Lewis was one of the number. The Indians retreated northward. Toward the close of each day when they found . . a pleasant spot which invited them to rest and feast, they lit their fires and celebrated their victory by the sacrifice of a captive."

be better to keep him with me, for he might be a Mean to get me clear much fooner."

The Officers belonging to Ofwego, would gladly have had me with them, but found it impracticable; this is an Inftance of Kindnefs and Condefcenfion, for which I am obliged! Captain Bradley, gave me a good Coat, Veft, and Shirt; and a young Gentleman, who formerly lived in Philadelphia, gave four Piftoles (his Name is James Stone, he was Doctor at Ofwego). Thefe generous Expreffions of Kindnefs and Humanity, I am under great Obligations to remember with affectionate Gratitude, and if ever it be in the Compafs of my Power,

---

and therefore flipt out of his Rank and concealed himfelf, by which Means, under God, he was preferved from a State of perpetual Captivity; his Place being filled up in his Abfence, the other unhappy Youths were delivered up a Sacrifice to the Indian Enemy, to be inftructed in Popifh Principles, and employed in Murdering their Countrymen; yea, perhaps, their Fathers and Brethren, O horrible! O lamentable! How can the French be guilty in cold Blood, of fuch prodigious Iniquity? Befides their infatiable Thirft of Empire, Doubtlefs the Pardons they get from their Pope, and their Priefts, embolden them, which brings to my Mind, what I faw when among them: On a Sabbaoth Day, perceiving a great Concourfe of People at a Chapel, built on the Commons, at fome Diftance from the City, I went to fee what was the Occafion, and found a kind of a Fair, at which were fold Cakes, Wine, Brandy, &c. I likewife faw many Carts and Chafes attending, the Chapel Doors in the mean Time open, Numbers of People going in and out, and a Board hanging over the Door, on which was written, in large Letters, INDULGENCE PLENARY, or FULL PARDON.

to requite: This Money, together with what my Son brought, I was in Hopes would go far towards procuring my Releaſe, from my Indian Maſters; but ſeeing a Number of Priſoners in ſore Diſtreſs, among which were, the Captains Grant and Shepherd,* and about Seven more in Company, I thought it my Duty to relieve them, and commit my Releaſe to the Diſpoſal of Providence! Nor was this ſuffered to turn to my Diſadvantage in the Iſſue, for my Deliverance was brought about in due Time, in another, and unexpected Way. This Company informed me of their Intention to Eſcape, accordingly I gave them all the Help in my Power, ſaw them clear of the Town, on a Saturday Evening, before the Centries were ſet at the Gates, and adviſed them not to part from each other, and delivered to Captain Shepherd two Pocket Compaſſes; but they contrary to this Counſel parted, and ſaw each other no more: By their ſeparating, Captain Grant, and Serjeant Newel, were deprived of the Benefit of a Compaſs; the other Part got ſafe to Fort William Henry, as I was informed by Serjeant Henry, who was brought in Priſoner, being taken in a Battle, when gallant, indefatigable Captain Rogers, made a brave Stand,

---

* Shepard was picked up by a scouting party that was under the active Major Robert Rogers. They had gone down Lake George on skates to look after French stragglers and examine the French posts.

againſt more than twice his Number! But I have not heard any Account of Captain Grant! Was enabled, through much Mercy, to continue communicating ſome Relief to other Priſoners, out of the Wages I received for my Labour, which was 40 Livers per Month!

In the latter Part of the Winter, Coal and Iron were ſo ſcarce, that I was hard ſet to get any more Work; I then offered to work for my Diet and Lodging, rather than be thruſt into a ſtinking Dungeon, or ſent among the Indians: The Interpreter took ſome Pains (which I thankfully acknowledge) but without Succeſs; however, as I offered to work without Wages, a Frenchman took me and my Son in, upon theſe Terms, till a better Birth preſented; here we ſtaid one Week, but heard of no other Place, then he offered me and my Son, 30 Livers per Month, to ſtrike and blow the Bellows, which I did for about two Months, and then was diſcharged, and traveled about from Place to Place, having no fixed Abode, and was obliged to lay out the ſmall Remains of my Caſh, in buying a little Victuals, and took a Hay-Loft for my Lodging: I then made my Caſe known to the kind Interpreter, and requeſted him to conſider of ſome Means for my Relief, who replied he would; in the mean Time, as I was taking a walk in the City, I met an Indian Priſoner, that belonged to the Town where my Father lived, who reported, that a great Part of the Indians there, were juft come, with a Refolution to carry me back with them; and knowing him to be a very honeft Fellow, I believed the Truth of it, and fled from the Town to be concealed from the Indians; in the mean while, Schemes were formed for an Efcape, and well profecuted: The Iffue of which was fortunate. General Vaudriel, gave me and my Son, Liberty (under his Hand) to go to Quebec, and work there at our Pleafure, without Confinement, as Prifoners of War; by which Means, I was freed from paying a Ranfom.

The Commiffary, Monfieur Partwe, being about to fet off for Quebec, my Son informed me that I muft come to Town in the Evening, a Paffage being provided for us; I waited till near Dark, and then entered the Town, with great Care, to efcape the Indians, who kept watch for me (and had done fo for fome Time) which made it very difficult and dangerous to move; however, as they had no Knowledge of my Son, he could watch their Motions, without their Sufpicion (the Providence of God is a great Deep, this Help was provided for my Extremity, not only beyond my Expectation, but contrary to my Defign.) In the Morning, upon feeing an Indian fet to watch for me, over againft the Houfe I was in, I quickly made my Efcape, through the back Part of the Houfe, over fome high Pickets, and out of the City, to the River Side, and fled!

A Friend knowing my Scheme for Deliverance, kindly affifted me to conceal myfelf: The Commiffary had by this Time got ready for his Voyage, of which my Son giving me Notice, I immediately, with no lingering Motion, repaired to the Boat, was received on board, fet off quite undifcovered, and faw the Indians no more! A very narrow and furprizing Efcape, from a violent Death! (For they had determined to kill me, in cafe I ever attempted to leave them) which lays me under the ftrongeft Obligations, to improve a Life refcued from the Jaws of fo many Deaths, to the Honour of my gracious Benefactor! — But to return, the Commiffary, upon feeing the Difmiffion I had from the General, treated us courteoufly! (g)

Arrived at Quebec, May 1ft, The honorable Colonel *Peter Schuyler,** hearing of my coming

---

g Saw many Houfes and Villages in our Pafs along the River St. Lawrence towards the Metropolis; and here it may be with Juftice obferved, that the Inhabitants of Canada in general, are principally (if not wholly) fettled upon Rivers, by reafon that their back Lands being flat and fwampy, are therefore unfit to bear Grain: Their Wheat is fown in the Spring of the Year, becaufe the Winter is long, and would drown it; they feem to have no good Notion of making Meadow (fo far as I had an Opportunity of obferving) their horned Cattle are few and poor, their Living in general mean, they eat but little Flefh, neverthelefs they are ftrong and hardy.

---

* Colonel Peter Schuyler. He was the son of Arent Schuyler, and both were notable men in the British colonies. The colonel was in command of a New Jersey regiment at Oswego when the French captured the place. "While a prisoner in

there, kindly fent for me, and after enquiries
about my Welfare, &c. generoufly told me I
fhould be fupplied, and need not trouble myfelf
for Support! This public fpirited Gentleman,
who is indeed an Honour to his Country, did
in like Manner, nobly relieve many other poor
Prifoners at Quebec! — Here I had full Liberty
to walk where I pleafed, and view the City,
which is well fituated for Strength, but far from
being impregnable.

Here, I hope, it will not be judged improper,
to give a fhort Hint of the French Governor's
Conduct; even in Time of Peace, he gives the
Indians great Encouragement to Murder and
Captivate the poor Inhabitants on our Frontiers;
an honeft, good Man, named William Rofs, was
taken Prifoner twice in the Time of Peace;
when he was firft taken, he learned a little of
the French Tongue, was after fome Time
redeemed, and got to his Place of Abode: Yet
fome Years after, he, with two Sons, was again
taken, and brought to Quebec; the Governor
feeing the poor Man was Lame, and one of his
Legs fmaller than the other, reproved the In-

Canada he kept open house for the relief of his fellow sufferers, and gave large sums to the Indians for the redemption of captives; many of whom he afterwards, at his own expense, maintained while there, and provided for their return, trusting to their abilities and honor for repayment; and lost considerable that way, but seemed to think it money well bestowed."
He lived at No. 1 Broadway, New York City, at one time.

dians for not killing him, afking, "what they brought a lame Man there for, who could do nothing but eat; you fhould, faid he, have brought his Scalp!" However, another of his Countrymen, more merciful than his Excellency, knowing the poor Prifoner to be a quiet, hard-working Man, redeemed him from the Indians; and two other Frenchmen bought his two Sons: Here they had been Slaves more than three Years, when I firft arrived at Quebec; this Account I had from Mr. Rofs himfelf, who farther added, that the Governor gave the Indians Prefents, to encourage them to proceed, in that kind of Work, which is a Scandal to any civilized Nation, and what many Pagans would abhor! Here alfo, I faw one Mr. Johnfon, who was taken in a Time of Peace, with his Wife, and three fmall Children (his Wife was big with Child of a Fourth, and delivered on the Road to Canada, which fhe called Captive *) all which, had been Prifoners between three and four Years, feveral young Men, and his Wife's Sifter, were likewife taken Captive with them, and made Slaves!

---

*Parkman refers to the daughter of John Smead and wife, as a child that was named "Captivity" under similar circumstances. The Smeads were captured when Fort Massachusetts was destroyed (1746). The child was born while they traveled through the woods. The Indians made a litter of poles and deerskins, placed mother and child on it, covered them with a bearskin, and then carried them on their way to the settlement in Canada.

Our Cartel being ready, I obtained Liberty to go to England in her; we ſet Sail the 23d of July, 1757, in the Morning, and diſcharged our Pilot about 4 o'Clock in the Afternoon; after which, we neither caſt Anchor or Lead, till we got clear of the great River St. Lawrence, from which, I conclude, the Navigation is much ſafer than the French have reported; in 28 Days we arrived at Plymouth, which occaſioned great Joy, for we were ragged, lowſy, ſick, and in a Manner, ſtarved; and many of the Priſoners, who in all were about 300 in Number, were ſick of the Small-Pox: My Son and Self, having each a Blanket Coat (which we bought in Canada to keep us warm) and now expecting Relief, gave them to two poor ſick Men, almoſt naked! But as we were not allowed to go on Shore, but removed to a King's Ship, and ſent to Portſmouth, where we were ſtill confined on board, near two Weeks, and then removed to the Mermaid,* to be ſent to Boſton; we now repented our well ment, though raſh Charity, in giving

---

*According to Allen's *Battles of the British Navy* the "Mermaid" was a 28-gun frigate. During our war of the Revolution the "Mermaid" fell in with the fleet under Count D'Estaing, as it was sailing up the American coast to attack General Howe, who was then (1778) in Philadelphia. The fleet went in chase of the "Mermaid," and drove her ashore on Cape Henlopen, but were thereby so much delayed in what was already an overlong passage, that Howe, and such few ships as were at Philadelphia, got clear of the Delaware.

our Coats away, as we were not to get any more, all Application to the Captain for any Kind of Covering being in vain; our Joy was turned into Sorrow, at the Profpect of coming on a cold Coaft, in the Beginning of Winter, almoft naked, which was not a little increafed, by a near View of our *Mother Country*, the Soil and Comforts of which, we were not fuffered to touch or tafte (h).

September the 6th, Set Sail for Bofton, with a Fleet in Convoy, at which we arrived on the Seventh of November, in the Evening; it being Dark, and we Strangers, and poor, it was difficult to get a Lodging (I had no Shoes, and but Pieces

---

h On board the Mermaid Man of War, being in a diftreffed Condition, and hearing little from the Mouths of many of my Countrymen, but Oaths and Curfes (which much increafed my Affliction) and finding it difficult to get a retired Place, I crept down into the Hold among the Water Casks, to cry to God; here the Lord was gracioufly pleafed to meet with me, and give me a Senfe of his fatherly Love and Care; here he enabled me (bleffed be his Name for ever) to look back and view how he had led me, and guarded me with a watchful Eye and ftrong Arm, and what Pains he had taken to wean me from an over-love of time Things, and make me content that he fhould choofe for me: Here I was enabled to fee his great Goodnefs in all my Difappointments, and that Afflictions were not Evidences of God's Wrath, but the Contrary, to all that honeftly Endeavour to feek him with Faith and Love; here I could fay, God is worthy to be ferved, loved, and obeyed, though it be attended with many Miferies in this World! What I have here mentioned, fo far as I know my heart, is neither to exalt myfelf, or offend any one upon Earth, but to glorify God, for his Goodnefs and Faithfulnefs to the Meaneft of his Servants, and to encourage others to truft in him!

of Stockings, and the Weather in the mean
Time very Cold) we were indeed directed to
a Tavern, but found cold Entertainment there,
the Mafter of the Houfe feeing a ragged and
lowfy Company, turned us out to Wander in the
Dark; he was fufpicious of us, and feared we
came from Halifax, where the Small-Pox then
was, and told us, he was ordered not to receive
fuch as came from thence: We foon met a
young Man, who faid he could find a Lodging
for us, but ftill detained us by afking many
Queftions; on which I told him we were in no
Condition to Anfwer, till we came to a proper
Place, which he quickly found, where we were
ufed well; but as we were lowfy, could not
expect Beds. The next Morning, we made
Application for Cloathing; Mr. Erwing, Son-in-
Law to the late General Shirley,* gave us Relief,

---

*William Shirley was governor of Massachusetts when this war began. After the conference with Braddock in Virginia Shirley was placed in command of the expedition that was to reduce Niagara. At Braddock's death he became commander-in-chief of the British forces in America, and he held that position at the time Eastburn was captured. It was by his orders that Fort Bull was filled with supplies, though but poorly garrisoned to resist a French invasion. He was an earnest, energetic, and capable civil officer, but was most unfortunate in this war, for his military enterprises failed, and he lost two sons in the army. Franklin in his autobiography says of him: "Tho' Shirley was not a bred soldier, he was sensible and sagacious in himself, and attentive to good advice from others, capable of forming judicious plans, and quick and active in carrying them into execution."

not only in refpect of Apparel, but alfo Three Dollars per Man, to bear our Charges to Newport: When I put on frefh Cloaths, I was feized with a cold Fit, which was followed by a high Fever, and in that Condition obliged to Travel on Foot, as far as Providence, in our Way to Rhode-Ifland (our Money not being fufficient to hire any Carriage, and find us what was needful for Support:) In this Journey, I was exceedingly diftreffed! Our Comforts in this Life, are often allaved with Miferies, which are doubtlefs great Mercies when fuitably improved; at Newport, met with Captain Gibbs, and agreed with him for our Paffage to New-York, where we arrived, November 21ft, met with many Friends, who expreffed much Satisfaction at our Return, and treated us kindly, particularly Meffrs. Livingfton, and Waldron.

November 26th, 1757. Arrived at Philadelphia, to the great Joy of all my Friends, and particularly of my poor afflicted Wife and Family, who thought they fhould never fee me again, till we met beyond the Grave; being returned, fick and weak in Body, and empty-handed, not having any Thing for my Family's and my own Support, feveral humane and generous Perfons, of different Denominations, in this City (without any Application of mine, directly or indirectly) have freely given feafonable Relief; for which, may God grant them

Bleſſings in this World, and in the World to come everlaſting Life, for Chriſt's ſake!

Now, God, in His great Mercy, hath granted me a temporal Salvation, and what is a Thouſand Times better, he hath given me with it, a Soul-ſatisfying Evidence of an eternal in the World to come!

And now, what ſhall I render to the Lord for all his Benefits, alas I am nonpluſt! O that Saints and Angels might praiſe thee, for I am not worthy to take thy Name into my Mouth any more! Yet notwithſtanding, thou art pleaſed to accept poor Endeavours, becauſe *Jeſus Chriſt* has opened the Door, whereby we may come boldly to the Throne of thy Grace, praiſed be the Lord God Jehovah, by Men and Angels, throughout all Eternity!

But to haſten to the Concluſion, ſuffer me with Humility and Sorrow to obſerve, that our Enemies ſeem to make a better Uſe of a bad Religion, than we of a good One; they riſe up long before Day in Winter, and go through the Snow in the coldeſt Seaſons, to perform their Devotions in the Churches; which when over, they return to be ready for their Work as ſoon as Day-Light appears: The Indians are as zealous in Religion, as the French, they oblige their Children to pray Morning and Evening, particularly at Conaſadauga; are punctual in performing their ſtated Acts of Devotion themfelves, are ftill and peaceable in their own Families, and among each other as Neighbours!

When I compared our Manner of Living with theirs, it made me fear that the righteous and jealous God (who is wont to make Judgment begin at his own Houfe firft) was about to deliver us into their Hands, to be feverely punifhed for our Departure from him; how long has he waited for our Return, O that we may therefore turn to him, before his Anger break out into a Flame, and there be no Remedy!

Our Cafe appears to me indeed very gloomy! notwithftanding our Enemies are inconfiderable in Number, compared with us; yet they are *united as one Man*, while we may be juftly compared to a Houfe divided againft itfelf, and therefore cannot ftand long, in our prefent Situation.

May Almighty God, gracioufly incline us to look to him for DELIVERANCE, to *repent* of our Sins, *reform* our Lives, and *unite* in the *vigorous* and *manly* Ufe of all proper Means to this End. Amen.

FINIS.

INDEX

ACADIA, British success in, 14.
Alexandria, Va., intercolonial conference at, 13.
Alleghany River, 11.
BRADDOCK, Gen. Edward, work of and defeat, 13.
Braddock, Pa., site of British defeat, 14.
Bradley, Capt., kind to Eastburn, 59.
"Britain, Old," eaten by Indians, 11.
Bull, Ft., attacked by French, 18-19; described, 32.

CANASADAUGA, described, 42, 45.
Captivity, name given to child born a prisoner on the trail, 65.
Cataraqui (Frontenac), Ft., account of, 53.
Céloron de Bienville, leads expedition to Ohio, 11.
Contrecœur, Capt., at forks of the Ohio, 12.
Coquard, Rev., describes Indian warfare, 15.
Crown Point to be attacked, 13, 17.

DEAD SHOUT, an Indian signal, 36.
Detroit, a French post, 11.
Dieskau, Baron, beaten at Lake George, 14.
Dinwiddie, Gov., opinion of traders, 10; opposes French invasion, 12; defends Virginia, 12, 13; evil he foresaw, 14.
Dumas, Capt., describes war, 14-15.
Duquesne, Ft., French post at forks of the Ohio, 13.
Duquesne, Gov., orders to, 14.

EASTBURN, Robert, birth, 7; converted, 7; as a trader, 9; to trade with Indians at Oswego, 15-16; stories of fight in which captured, 16; follows scouting party, 29; captured and robbed, 30; prevents attack on Ft. Williams, 31; at capture of Ft. Bull, 32; sufferings on way to Canada, 33 et seq.; reaches Oswegotchie, 38; down the St. Lawrence, 39; ordered to dance the prisoners' song 40; leaves the St. Lawrence, 41; in a French settlement 42; at Canasadauga, 43; runs the gauntlet, 44; adopted into Indian family and ordered to Oswegotchie, 45; an Indian feast that was not relished, 46; refuses to go tc mass, 47; at work in woods 48; sent to Montreal, 49, hears Oswego is to be attacked, 50; describes French methods with Indians, 51; on return to Oswegotchie thinks to escape, 52; at work fortifying Oswegotchie, plot to escape fails, sent to Cohnewago, 54; at work at trade, meets Mary Harris, starts for Montreal, 55; when Oswego was captured, 56; meets his son among the prisoners, 57; describes son's adventures as a prisoner, 58; refused permission to go to Quebec, 58; helps prisoners to escape, 60; works with son for a French smith, 61; permitted to go with son to Quebec, escapes from the Indians, 62-63; describes settlements on way to Quebec, 63; aided by Col. Peter Schuyler, 63-64; sent in cartel to England, 66; returns to Boston in frigate "Mermaid," 66-67; distressful condition, 67-68; relieved by Erwing, son-in-law of Gov. Shirley, 68-69; at New York, meets prominent people, 69; at home, 69 *et seq.*

Erie, Pa.. on French route to the Ohio, 11.

Erwing, Mr., son-in-law of Gov. Shirley, kind to Eastburn, 68.

FRONTENAC (Cataraqui), Ft., account of, 53.

GRANT, Captain, a prisoner, escapes from French, 62.

HAMILTON, Gov., opinion of traders, 10.

Harris, Mary, account of, 55.

JOHNSON, Gen. Wm., checks French, 14; sends force in chase of Léry, 33.

Johnson, Mr., a prisoner well treated by Indians, 65.

Jumonville, Ensign, attacked by Washington, 12.

LA CHINE, story of, 52.

Langlade, Chas., a French trader, attacks Pickawillany, 9, 11.

La Salle, first exploration mentioned, 54.

Le Bœuf, French post, 11.

Legardeur de St. Pierre, reply to Washington, 12.

Léry, Joseph Chaussegros de, commands expedition to head of Mohawk Valley, 17-19; record, 32.

INDEX

Lewis, Francis, account of, when taken prisoner at Oswego, 58.

MERMAID, British frigate, account of, 66.

Mohawk River, in route to Oswego, 29.

Mohawk-Wood Creek carrying-place, 7, 17, 18.

Montresor, James, an engineer, 29.

Mount Calvary, mission described, 45.

NECESSITY, FORT, captured by French, 13.

Newel, Serjeant, a prisoner among French, 60.

Niagara, to be attacked, 13, 17,

OGDENSBURG, on site of Oswegotchie, 18.

Oswego, N.Y., frontier trading-post, 8, 29; origin, 33; threatened, 50, 53; captured, 56.

Oswegotchie (Ogdensburg), site of French mission, 18; described, 38.

PICKAWILLANY, an Indian settlement, 9, 11.

Piquet, Abbé, work as missionary, 45; record, 49–50; at Oswegotchie, 53.

Pittsburg, site of fort, 12.

Porcupine, as food, and habits, 35.

Prisoners' song, Eastburn refuses to dance, 40, 44.

QUEBEC, mentioned, 32; destination of prisoners taken at Oswego, 58; Eastburn's life at, 63 *et seq*.

RAYMOND, commandant on Maumee, letter on English Indian trade, 11.

Rogers, Maj. Robert, scouting down Lake George, 60.

Rome, N. Y., at site of trail where Eastburn was captured, 7.

ST. LAWRENCE RIVER, described, 41.

Schuyler, Col. Peter, account of, 63–64.

Seven Years' War, described, 9 *et seq.;* situation of French in 1756, 17.

Shepherd, Capt., a prisoner, escapes from French, 60.

Shirley, Gov. William, opposes French, 13; account of, 68.

Smead, John, and wife, well treated as prisoners, 65.

Stanwix, Ft., location, 29.

Stone, Dr., assists Eastburn, 59.

TICONDEROGA, French post, 17.

Traders, Indian, described, 8, 10.

Treaty, Utrecht, mentioned, 10; Aix-la-Chapelle, mentioned, 10.

Trent, Wm., to build fort at forks of the Ohio, 12.

VAUDREUIL, Gov., plans attacks on English, 17; receives Eastburn, 49; and the Oneidas,

50–51; allows Eastburn to go to Quebec, 62; inhumanity of, 64–65.

Venango, Pa., on French route to the Ohio, 12.

Villiers, Coulon de, captures Ft. Necessity, 13.

WASHINGTON, Geo., a messenger to the French, 12; attacks Jumonville, 12; driven from Ft. Necessity, 13.

Waterford, site of Le Bœuf, 11.

William, Ft., head of Mohawk, 18; described, 29.

Williams, Capt. W., commands Ft. William, 29.

William Henry, Ft., mentioned, 60.

Whitefield, Rev. George, described by Franklin, 8.

Wood Creek, in route to Oswego, 29.

www.ingramcontent.com/pod-product-compliance
Lightning Source LLC
Chambersburg PA
CBHW051704090426
42736CB00013B/2530